How to Enjoy the Weather

by Jonny Walker
Illustrated by Nadja Sarell

Say the sounds.

/s/	-ce *as in dance*
/e/	-ea *as in bread*
/u/	o *as in onion*
/d/	-ed *as in rained*
/t/	-ed *as in dropped*

Blend the sounds to read the words.

son	weather	cover
bounce	drenched	kicked

Are you ready for all seasons?

I will look them up!

Get ready for different weather.

The seasons 🔍

Spring feels breezy and fresh.
New things grow. It gets a
bit hotter.

What might
I see?

newborn goats **bleating** ✓

flowers **blossoming** ✓

cloudless skies ✓

My son has picked some bright yellow flowers!

Summer is the hot season.
The days grow long.

How can I protect myself from the sun?

spread suncream on ✅

enjoy chilled drinks ✅

cover up the skin ✅

It is fun to play in the sun!

In this season, things get a little cooler. Expect heavy rain, too!

How might I enjoy that?

eat pumpkin stew ☑

jump about in puddles ☑

play with leaf pictures ☑

kick the leaves ☑

Lots of choices.
I kicked the wet
puddle. Now, I am
drenched!

Winter is the chilly season. The ground may get covered in snow.

What do I need?

 **earmuffs** ✅

 fleece or jumper ✅

 mittens ✅

 a thick coat ✅

I love it when it snows!

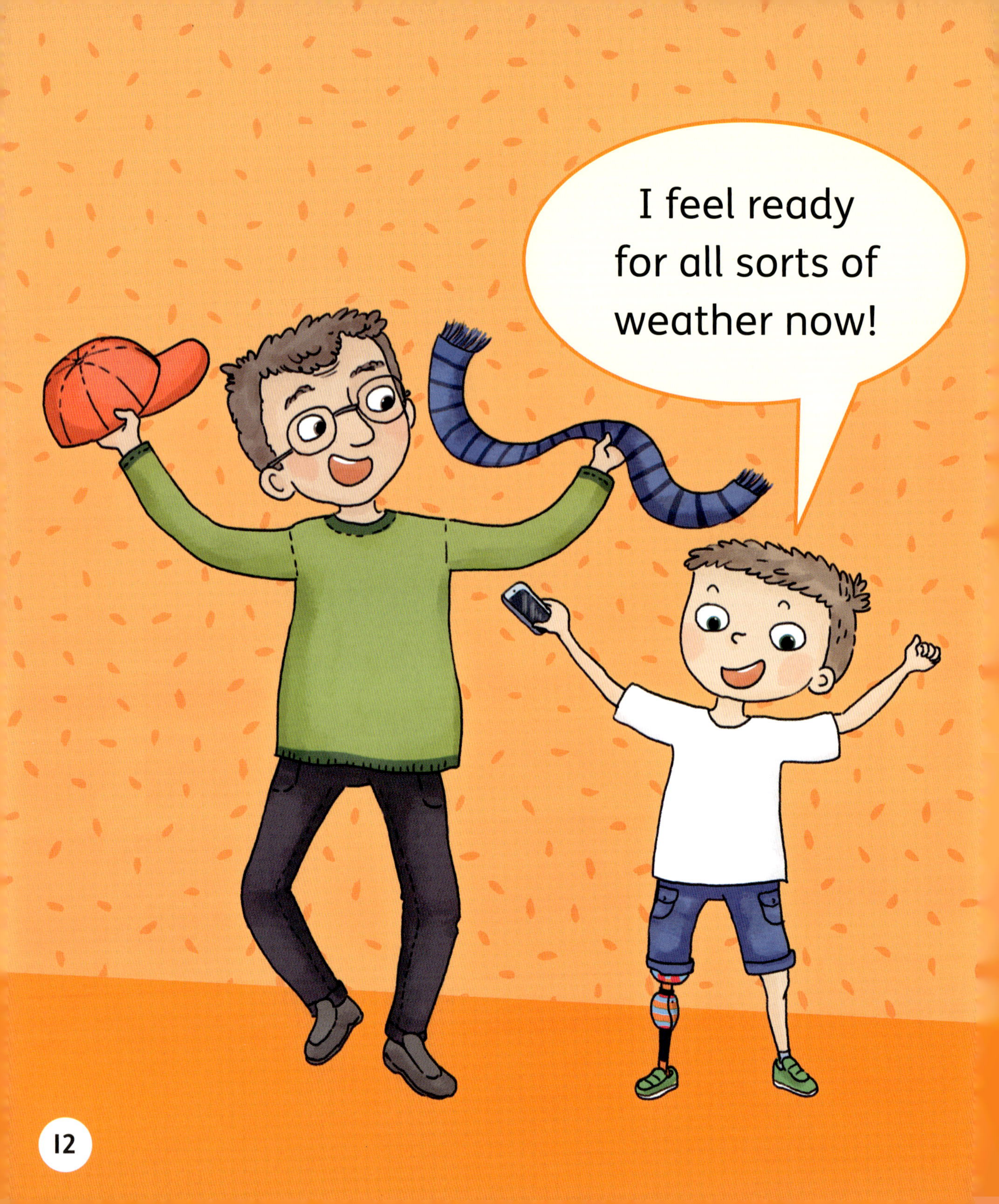
I feel ready for all sorts of weather now!

It is a hot, sunny day. My paddling pool is pumped up.

I will bounce and splash in it!

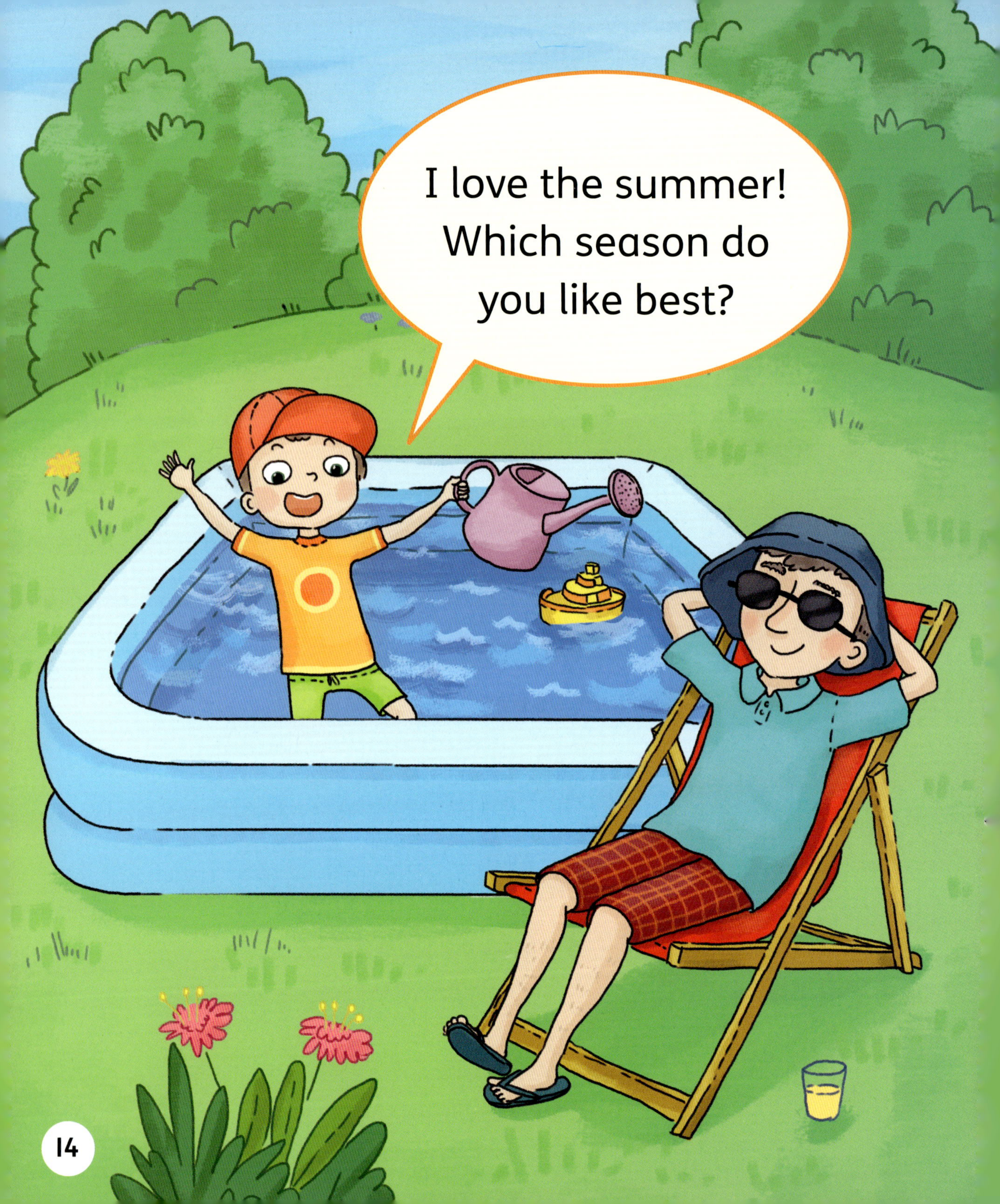
I love the summer! Which season do you like best?

Glossary

bleating: the crying sound of a goat kid

blossoming: starting to flower

earmuffs: protect ears from the chill

drenched: very wet

Talk together

1. Which season happens after spring?

2. What do people wear in winter?

3. Match the clothes to the seasons.

AFTER READING

Focus on phonics

- Look for words in the book that contain the /s/ sound in different spellings, e.g. *seasons, bounce.*
- Find words in the book with the 'ed' ending that make the /d/ sound or the /t/ sound, e.g. *covered, drenched.*

Think about the story

- Ask your child to tell you the key points that they've learned about this topic.
- Ask them how they can protect themselves in the sun.
- Ask them to explain what the word 'drenched' means.

OXFORD
UNIVERSITY PRESS

Great Clarendon Street, Oxford, OX2 6DP, United Kingdom

Oxford University Press is a department of the University of Oxford. It furthers the University's objective of excellence in research, scholarship, and education by publishing worldwide. Oxford is a registered trade mark of Oxford University Press in the UK and in certain other countries

Text © Oxford University Press 2022

Inside cover notes written by Suzy Ditchburn

The moral rights of the author have been asserted

First published 2022

British Library Cataloguing in Publication Data

Data available

ISBN: 978-1-382-03061-8

10 9 8 7 6 5 4 3 2 1

Paper used in the production of this book is a natural, recyclable product made from wood grown in sustainable forests. The manufacturing process conforms to the environmental regulations of the country of origin.

Printed in China by Shanghai Offset Printing Products Ltd.

Acknowledgements

With thanks to Debbie Hepplewhite

The publisher and author would like to thank the following for permission to use photographs and other copyright material:

Front Cover: Happy Together / Shutterstock; Yuganov Konstantin / Shutterstock; **Back Cover:** OlgaGi / Shutterstock. **Photos: p3(tl):** 1000 Words / Shutterstock; **p3(tr):** Sarah Jane Taylor / Shutterstock; **p3(bl):** Andrew Zarivny / Shutterstock; **p3(br):** PJ_Photography / Shutterstock; **p4:** 1000 Words / Shutterstock; **p5(t):** imagevixen / Shutterstock; **p5(m):** Andrew Balcombe / Shutterstock; **p5(b):** loskutnikov / Shutterstock; **p6(bgr):** Sarah Jane Taylor / Shutterstock; **p7(t):** DaniloAndjus / Getty Images; **p7(m):** Yuliia Sihurko / Shutterstock; **p7(b):** airdone / Shutterstock; **p8:** Andrew Zarivny / Shutterstock; **p9(t):** MNStudio / Shutterstock; **p9(mt):** alenka2194 / Shutterstock; **p9(mb):** Tomsickova Tatyana / Shutterstock; **p9(b):** Westend61/ Getty Images; **p10:** PJ_Photography / Shutterstock; **p11(t):** петр корчмарь / Alamy Stock Photo; **p11(b):** OlgaGi / Shutterstock; **p11(mt):** OlgaGi / Shutterstock; **p11(mb):** Mitrofanova / Shutterstock; **p15(l):** Infocugal / Shutterstock; **p15(r):** Artsplav / Shutterstock; **p15(m):** FamVeld / Shutterstock; **p16(tl):** Sarah Jane Taylor / Shutterstock; **p16(tr):** Mitrofanova / Shutterstock; **p16(ml):** PJ_Photography / Shutterstock; **p16(mr):** alenka2194 / Shutterstock; **p16(bl):** Andrew Zarivny / Shutterstock; **p16(br):** airdone / Shutterstock.

Illustrated by Nadja Sarell.

Every effort has been made to contact copyright holders of material reproduced in this book. Any omissions will be rectified in subsequent printings if notice is given to the publisher.

Oxford OWL Discover eBooks, inspirational resources, advice and professional development www.oxfordowl.co.uk

Floppy's Phonics
Decoding Practice

Oxford
Level 4

Book Band Light Blue

How to Enjoy the Weather

Are you ready for all the seasons?

/s/	s	-ce
/e/	e	-ea
/u/	u	o
-ed	/d/	/t/

Books at **Level 4**

The Camping Trip
Fantastic Things from th
  Soil
Roy Digs and Digs
Plastic in the Seas
What is in the Shed?
> **How to Enjoy the Weatl**

OXFORD
UNIVERSITY PRESS

web   www.oxfordprimary.co.uk
email primary.enquiries@oup.com
tel.   +44 (0) 1536 452610

ISBN 978-1-382-03061

9 781382 030618